UNDERWATER

That's Gross!
A Look at Science

Julie Murray

Big Buddy BOOKS
That's Gross!

VISIT US AT
www.abdopublishing.com

Published by ABDO Publishing Company, 8000 West 78th Street, Edina, Minnesota 55439.

Coordinating Series Editor: Rochelle Baltzer
Editor: Sarah Tieck
Contributing Editors: Marcia Zappa
Graphic Design: Deborah Coldiron
Cover Photograph: *Brandon Cole Marine Photography:* Brandon Cole; *iStockPhoto:* Michal Rozanski; *Photos.com:* Jupiter Images.
Interior Photographs/Illustrations: *AnimalsAnimals-Earth Scenes:* F. Ehrenstrom/OSF (p. 11), Tim Rock (p. 21); *Brandon Cole Marine Photography:* Brandon Cole (pp. 7, 9, 19, 25, 30); *Earthwindow.com:* Mike Johnson (p. 23); *iStockPhoto:* Carlos Alvarez (p. 15), Joe Belanger (p. 17), Jani Bryson (pp. 10, 17, 26), Christian Carroll (p. 29), Jacek Chabraszewski (p. 14), Eric Delmar (p. 23), Silke Dietze (p. 29), David Hernandez (p. 30), iStockPhoto (p. 15, 25), Bonnie Jacobs (p. 9), Bela Tibor Kozma (p. 7), Cat London (p. 28), Nancy Nehring (p. 15), Mike Sonnenberg (pp. 13, 18), Dane Steffes (p. 29); *Minden Pictures:* Fred Bavendam (p. 27), Flip Nicklin (p. 13); *Photos.com:* Jupiter Images (pp. 5, 7, 15); Simeon Dwyer (p. 19).

Library of Congress Cataloging-in-Publication Data

Murray, Julie, 1969-
  Underwater / Julie Murray.
    p. cm. -- (That's gross! A look at science)
  ISBN 978-1-60453-558-7
  1. Marine animals--Juvenile literature. I. Title.

QL122.2.M87 2009
591.77--dc22
                                        2008036383

Contents

Exploring Underwater

The world underwater is amazing! It is full of bright colors and unusual creatures. Look a little closer. You'll see that behind all that cool stuff is a lot of yuck. Some of it is natural. Some of it is unhealthy. Let's explore!

A Star Is Born

Starfish have very strange bodies. Most starfish can **regenerate** (rih-JEH-nuh-rayt). So if a starfish loses a body part, it can grow back!

Some say unknowing sailors used to chop up pesky starfish. Then, they would throw them back into the sea. However, this didn't always kill the starfish. Sometimes, it made even more! That's because some starfish **reproduce** (ree-pruh-DOOS) by regenerating.

Harlequin shrimp hunt starfish and slowly eat them alive. Some even feed starfish to keep them alive longer! They eat the new body parts as the starfish grows them.

This starfish lost an arm. A new one can grow in its place.

Sea sponges can regenerate, too!

The underside of a starfish is covered in tiny tube feet. These strong little **suction** (SUHK-shuhn) cups help them hold on to surfaces, such as rocks. The suction is very strong. Sometimes, a starfish's feet may tear off and remain stuck!

Starfish have two stomachs. Many starfish eat animals with shells, such as clams. Starfish use their suction feet to force open clamshells. Then, they push one stomach into the shell to **digest** the clam.

To eat a clam, a starfish pushes its stomach through its mouth and into the clam. When it is done eating, it pulls its stomach back inside its body.

Psssssst . . .
Sometimes starfish eat other starfish!

9

Mean and Ugly

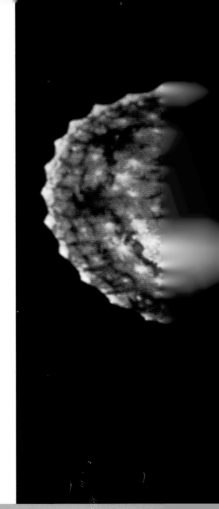

The anglerfish is one ugly fish. Some have big, staring eyes. Others are called "allmouth" because of their wide mouth filled with sharp teeth.

Most anglerfish have **lures** on their heads. This helps them catch fish. When a fish gets close, an anglerfish swallows it whole!

Really?

Some types of male anglerfish can't live on their own. The male attaches himself to a female by biting her. In time, his body becomes part of hers. His eyes, teeth, and organs disappear!

10

If a fish bites off an anglerfish's lure, some anglerfish can grow another one.

Want a Drink?

Underwater animals poop and pee in the water. Animals also give birth and die in the water. Some animals shed skin, mucus (MYOO-kuhs), and body parts. Yuck!

But water moves, flows, and empties. This naturally helps keep the water clean and healthy.

Water is full of plankton. Plankton is made up of tiny drifting plants and animals. Scientists call the animals zooplankton. The plants are known as phytoplankton.

When water stops moving, it becomes stagnant. Stagnant water can be smelly and dirty. **Bacteria** (bak-TIHR-ee-uh) and **parasites** (PEHR-uh-sites) often grow there. This makes the water unhealthy for living things.

Sometimes harmful matter, garbage, and even human waste gets into water. This is called pollution. When rivers, oceans, and lakes can't clean themselves fast enough, plants and animals die. The water becomes unsafe for people to touch and drink, too.

Algae (AL-jee) are plantlike organisms often found in stagnant water. Some algae grow in tight clumps that can kill fish and make water unsafe for humans.

One type of pollution is oil. When oil spills into water, it spreads all over the water's surface. Animals and plants may get very sick and die.

Pesky mosquitoes (muh-SKEE-tohs) lay their eggs in stagnant water.

What's for Dinner?

Octopuses have nasty ways of getting their dinner. Some can poison their **prey**. Poison from an octopus can make an animal unable to move.

Some octopuses like to eat animals with shells, such as clams. One way an octopus does this is by using its rough beak to make a hole in the shell. Then, it spits poison into the shell. This turns the animal's body into liquid goo. Finally, the octopus sucks out its dinner, like it is drinking with a straw!

An octopus's eight arms are helpful for eating clams. An octopus uses these ar to hold a clamshell while making a hole

For real?

Octopuses like to hunt at night. Some even eat other octopuses!

How Egg-citing!

Laying eggs is gooey, gloppy work. Some anglerfish lay their eggs in slimy, jellylike sheets. These sheets may hold more than 1 million eggs! They float in the ocean **currents**.

Octopuses lay eggs, too. Their soft eggs are oval, like tiny white grapes. Some mother octopuses hang the eggs together in long strings. These strings can have 100 or more eggs!

A female octopus may have thousands of eggs in her den!

Crayfish carry their eggs under their tails. They look like rotting, brown raspberries. Yuck!

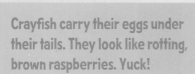

Spill Your Guts

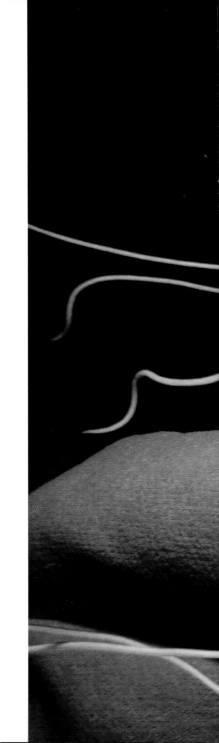

The ocean can be a very unsafe place. Each sea creature must have a way to guard itself.

Some sea cucumbers guard themselves in a very gross way. When they sense a predator, they shoot out their guts! This allows them to escape. These sea cucumbers quickly grow new guts.

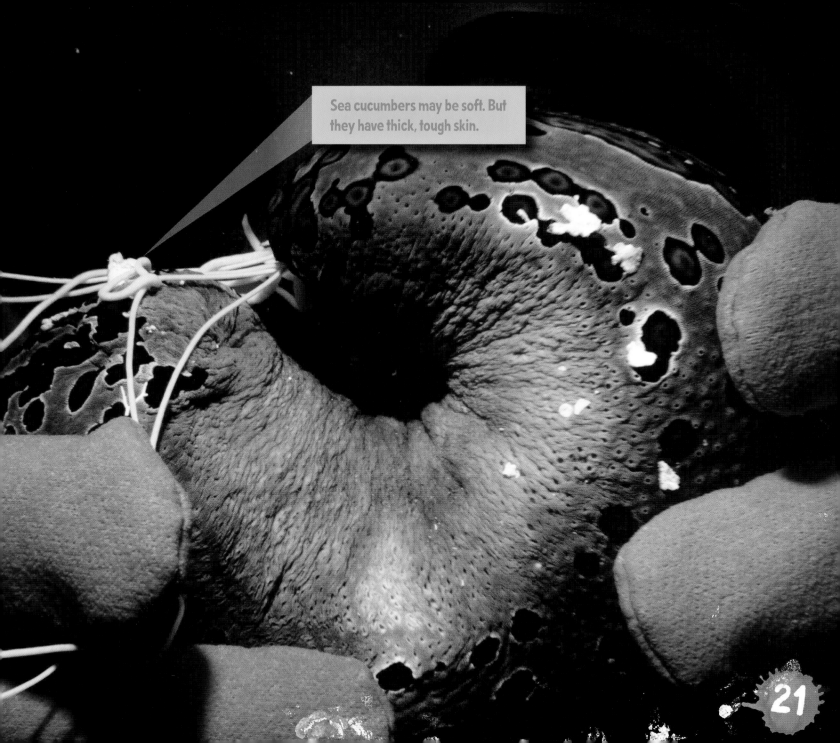

Sea cucumbers may be soft. But they have thick, tough skin.

Dinner Date

Parasites live off of other animals. Sometimes they hold on to the **host**'s body. Other times, they live inside it.

The ocean sunfish may have up to 40 kinds of parasites living on its body! It stays near the water's surface. That way, birds and other fish can eat off the parasites. Gross!

Humans can get parasites, too. Parasites spread through foods, drinks, and bug bites. They often make people very sick.

22

Smaller fish help keep ocean sunfish clean by eating off parasites.

An Ocean Sunfish Parasite

One Gross Fish

The hagfish is ugly, pink, and covered with a layer of mucus. This slimy coating helps guard hagfish. It is hard for predators to catch them because they are so slippery!

When a hagfish has too much slime, it ties itself up in a knot (NAHT). Then, it slides the knot down its body to push off mucus.

24

Hagfish are bottom dwellers. Most live on soft, muddy ocean floors.

The hagfish likes to eat sick or dead animals. This is called scavenging (SKA-vuhnj-ihng). The hagfish roots around inside the dead bodies for its meal. It starts on the inside and eats its way out. Yuck!

Many other animals, such as some crabs, are also scavengers.

27

That WAS Gross!

Between gooey eggs, slimy hagfish, and stinky pollution, some very yucky things are underwater.

Now that you know about all the grossness, take a closer look! Many gross things are just a part of life and no big deal. Others can be prevented. Do what you can to live in a healthy way!

28

Sometimes, people litter near water. If you see trash that is safe to pick up, put it in a garbage can. This helps keep water clean for plants and animals.

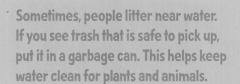

There's a limited amount of usable water in the world. To prevent wasting it, take short showers. And, don't run the water while you brush your teeth or soap up your hands.

Dog poop can pollute water. So if you have a dog, pick up its poop! Dirty water can make people and animals sick.

Eeeeww! What is THAT?

Answer on page 32.

30

Important Words

bacteria tiny one-celled organisms that can only be seen through a microscope. Some are germs.

current the flow and movement of a large body of water.

digest to break down food into parts small enough for the body to use.

host a living animal or plant on or in which a parasite lives.

knot a tightly twisted lump or connection.

lure a fleshy growth used to draw in animals for capture.

mucus thick, slippery, protective fluid from the body.

parasite a living thing that lives in or on another living thing. It gains from its host, which it usually hurts.

prey an animal hunted or killed by another animal, or predator, for food.

regenerate the act of replacing lost or hurt body parts.

reproduce to produce offspring.

shed to cast aside or lose as part of a natural process of life.

suction the act or process of drawing out using force.

Web Sites

To learn more about gross stuff, visit ABDO Publishing Company online. Web sites about gross stuff are featured on our Book Links page. These links are routinely monitored and updated to provide the most current information available.

Index

"Eeeeww! What Is THAT?" answer: octopus eggs.